Dale and Gail will sail in a race.

2

Dale zips up and wades in the lake.
Dale is safe for the race.

Gail zips up and gets set to sail.
Dale pulls up the main sail.

3

4

A big wind rips the sail.
Dale's tape will save the day!

Dale and Gail gain in the race.
Will a big wave get Dale and Gail wet?

5

6

Gail bails with a pail.
Dale made a pail with the tape.
Dale and Gail bail and bail.

But wait! Dale gets a fan.
Dale and Gail can tame the lake!

7

8 Dale and Gail get to the gate.
Will Dale and Gail win the race?